This Candlewick Studio book belongs to

Dive, Dive into the Night Sea

Thea Lu

CANDLEWICK STUDIO
an imprint of Candlewick Press

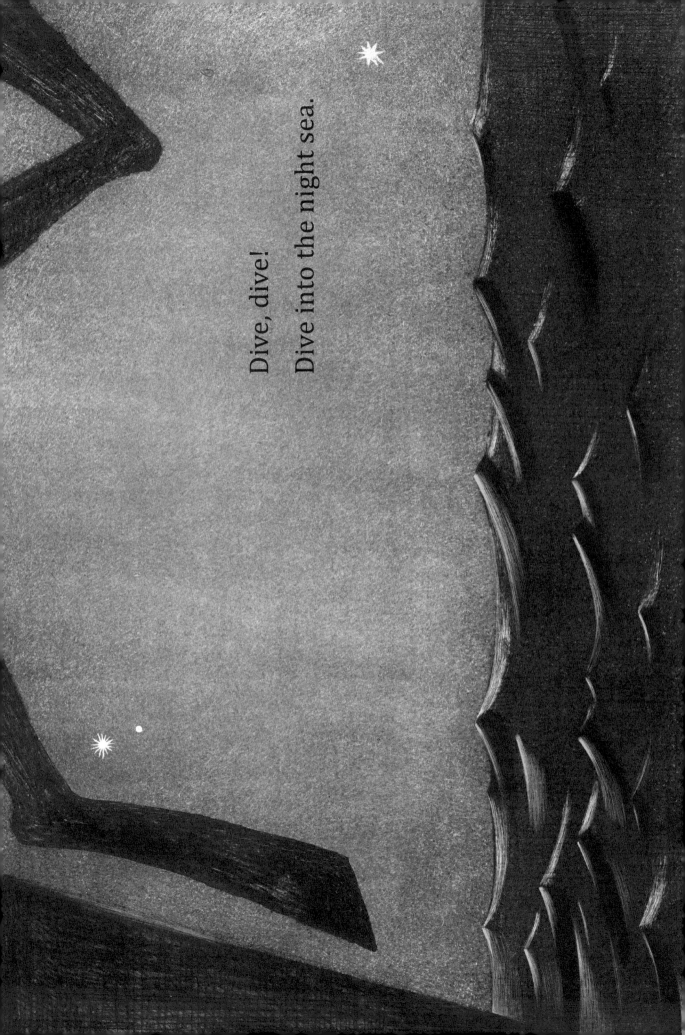

Dive, dive!
Dive into the night sea.

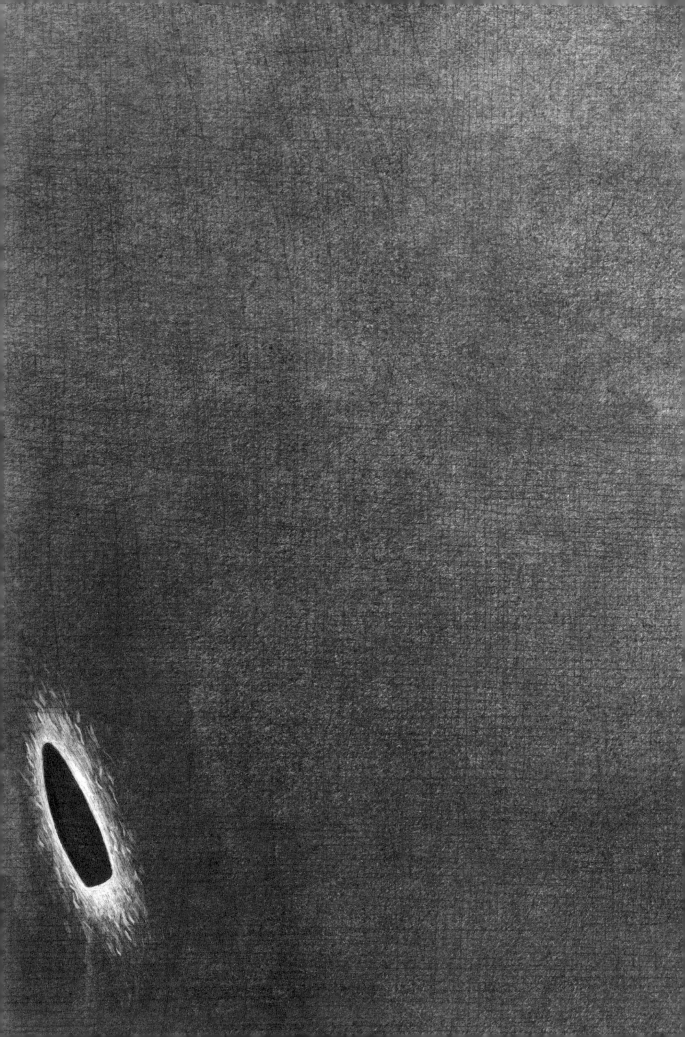

Dive into the inky depths.

It's usually busy down here during the day. Where has everybody gone?

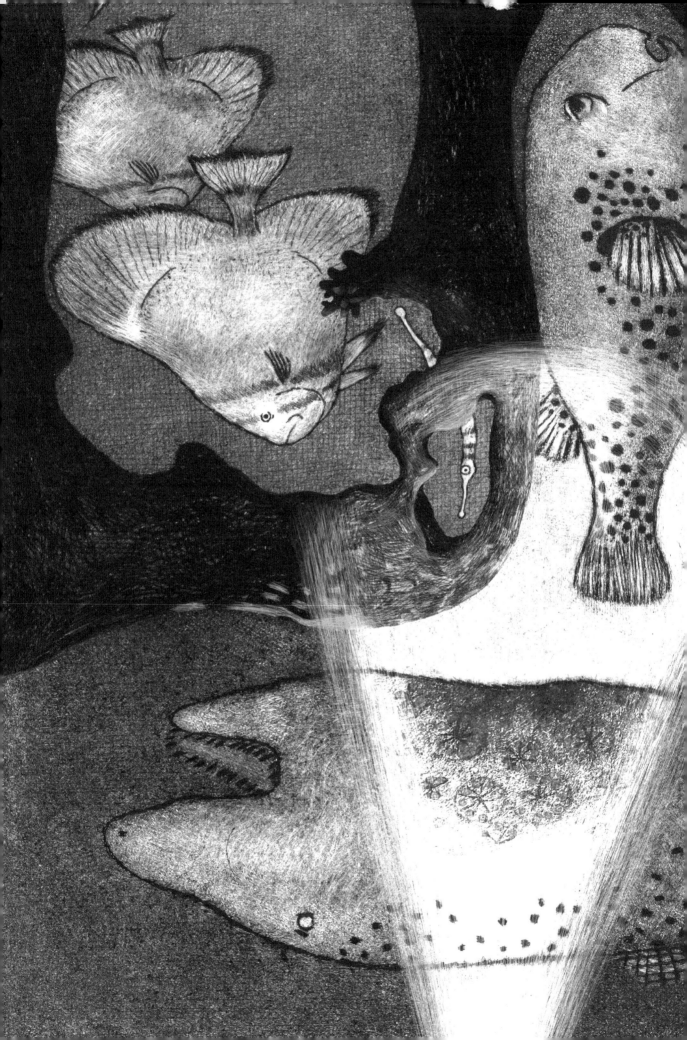

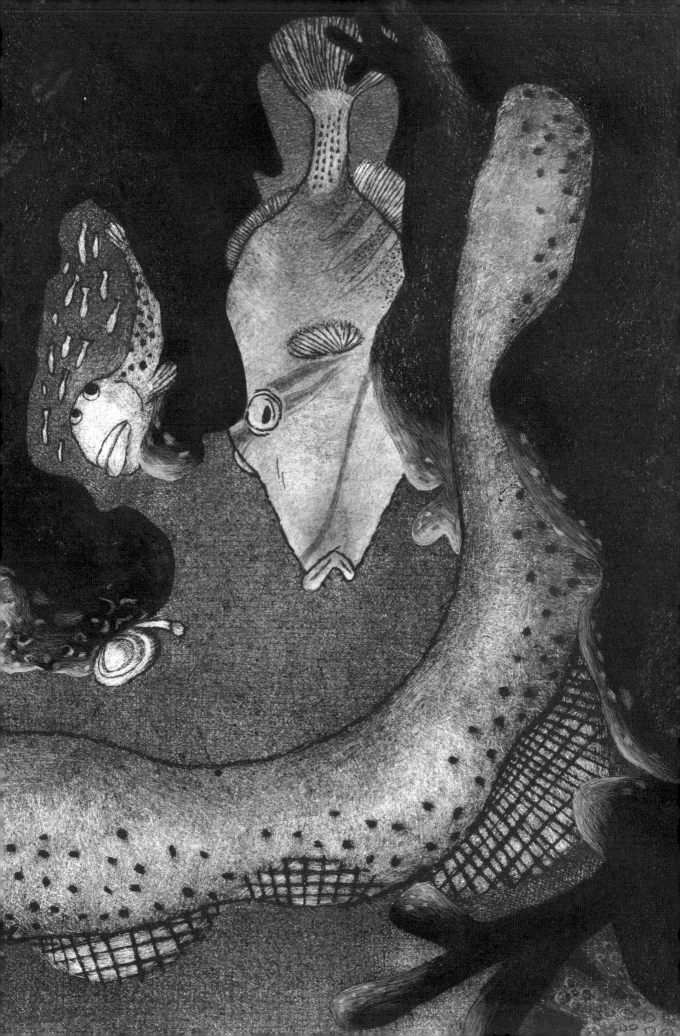

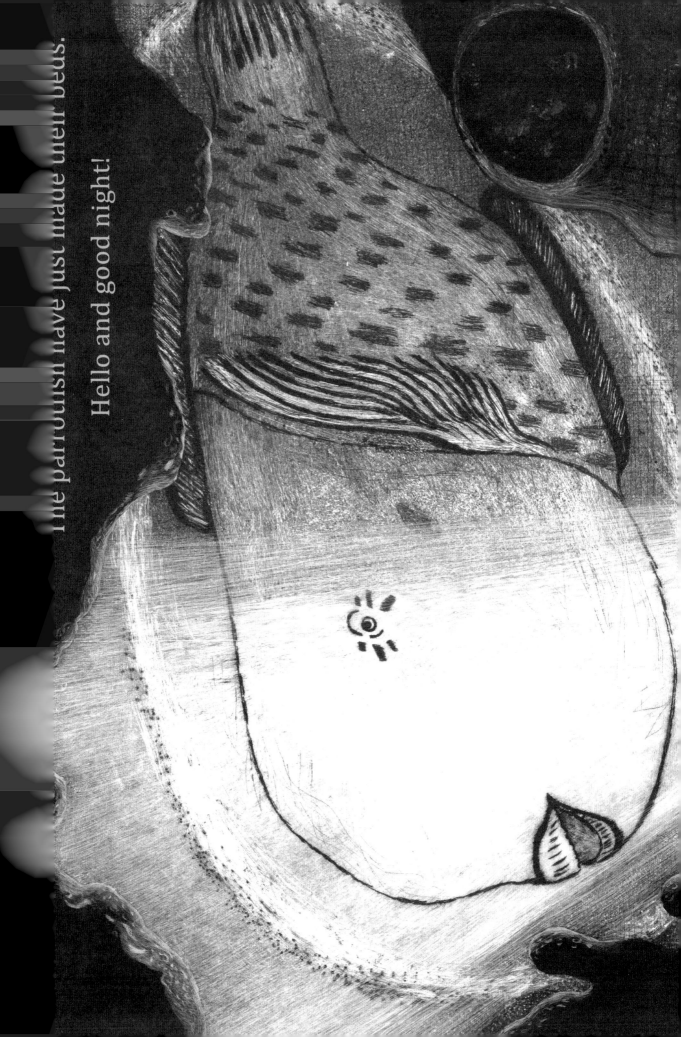

The parrotfish have just made their beds.

Hello and good night!

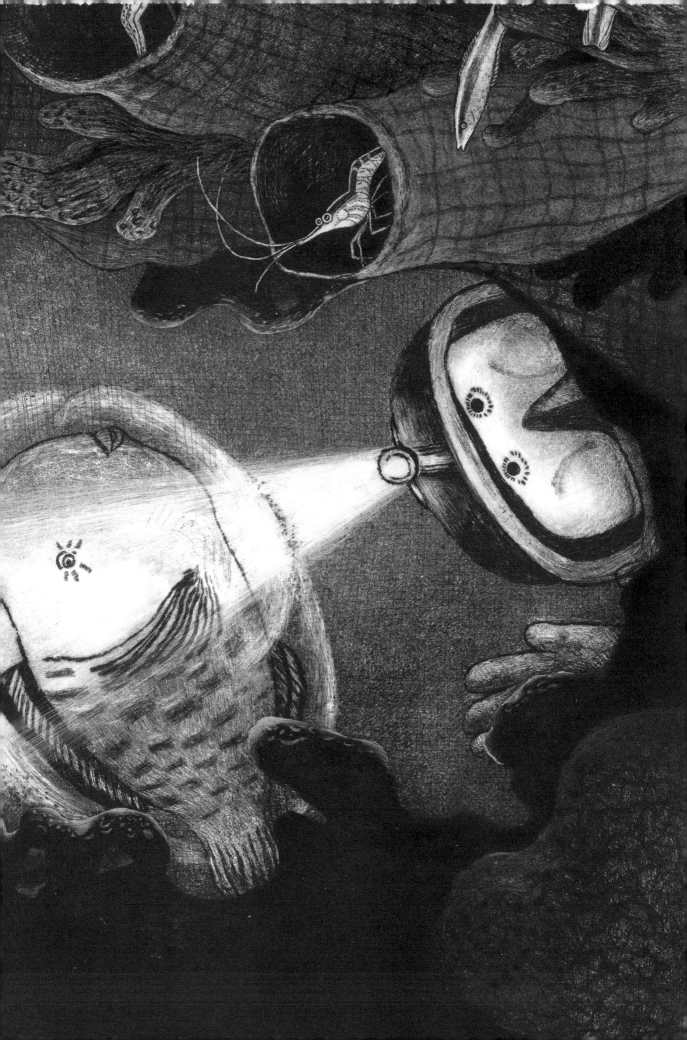

Dive, dive!
Dive into the night sea.

I shine my light and wait
to see who will come to me.

It's hard to resist a glimmer of light
in the darkness. Some little ones
come to say hello ....

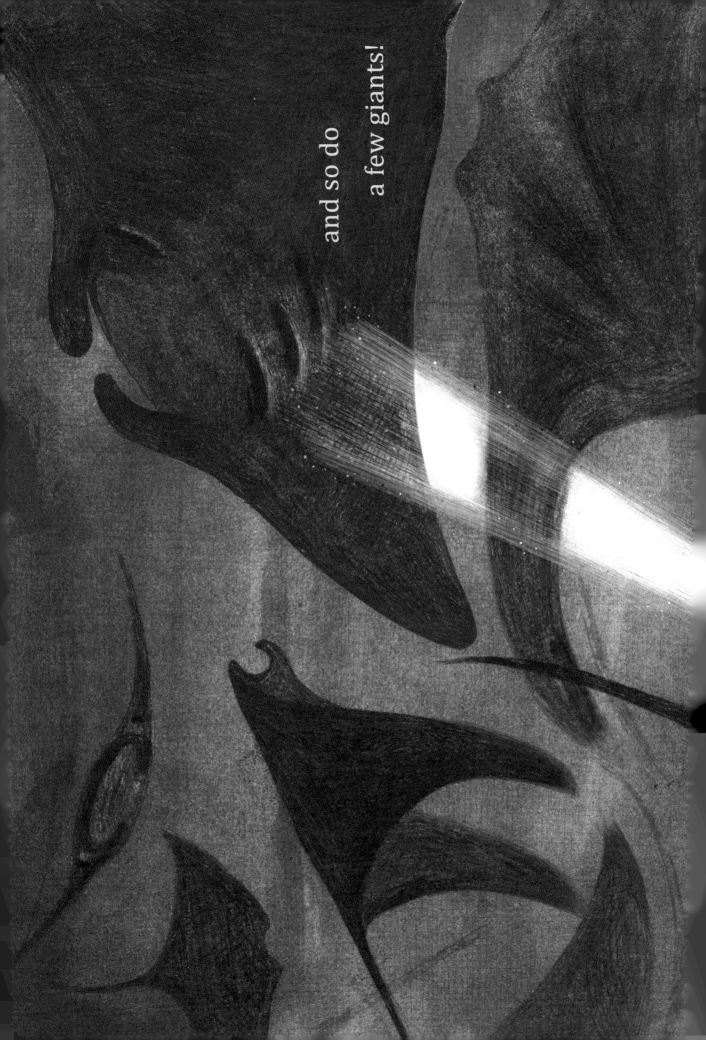

and so do
a few giants!

If I'm brave enough
to turn off my light,
how will the night sea reward me?

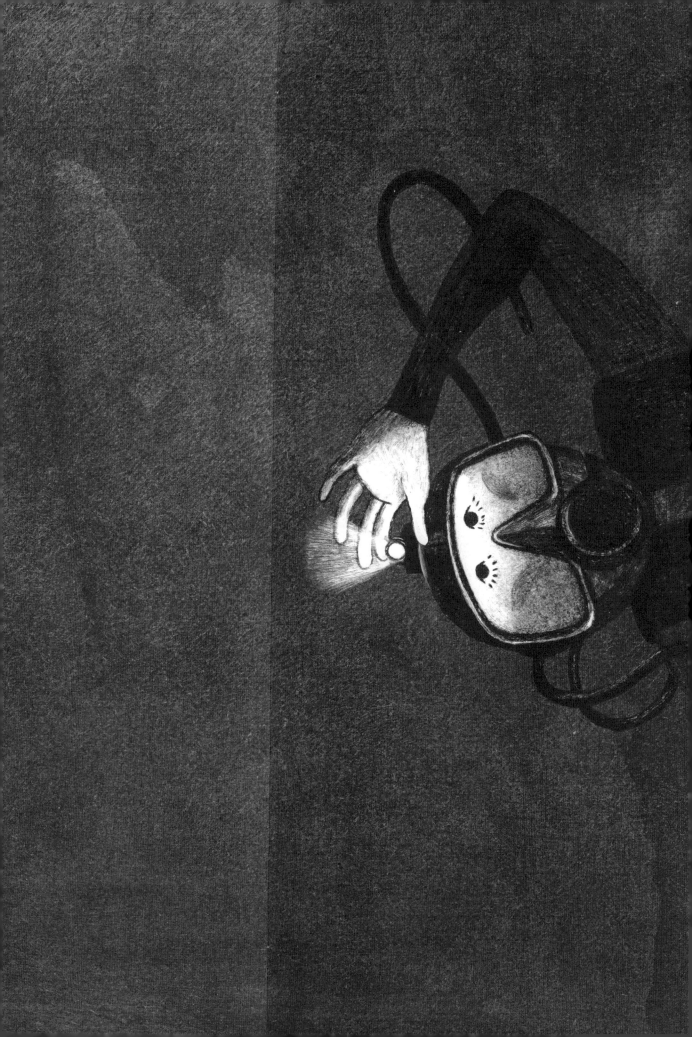

a constellation of stars
appears all around me!

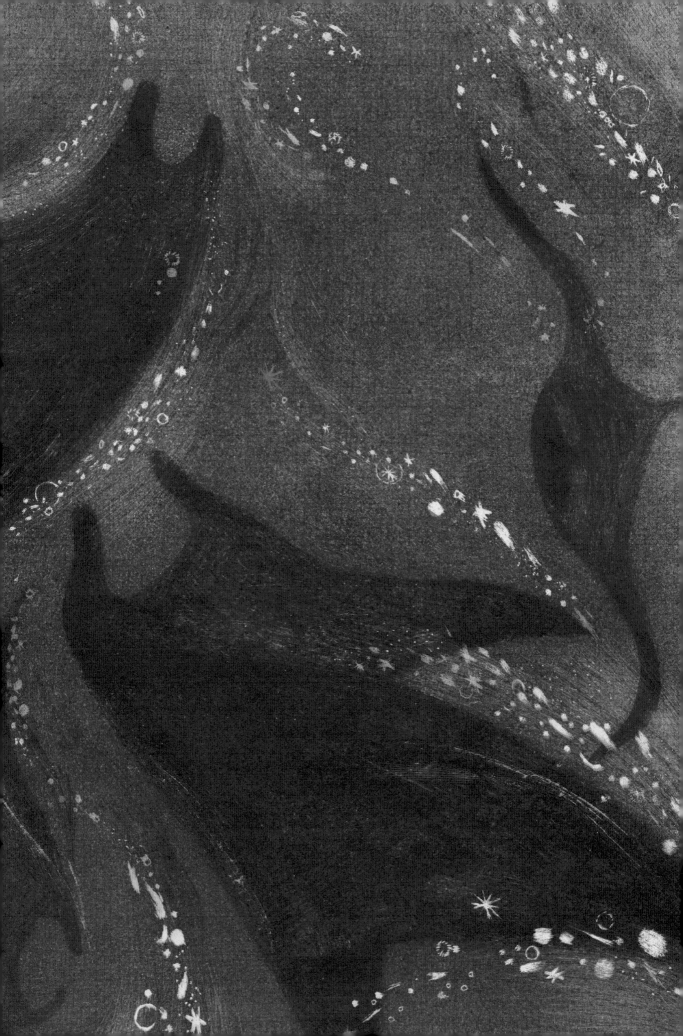

The world of the night sea

is like a beautiful dream.

But the time has come for me to leave.

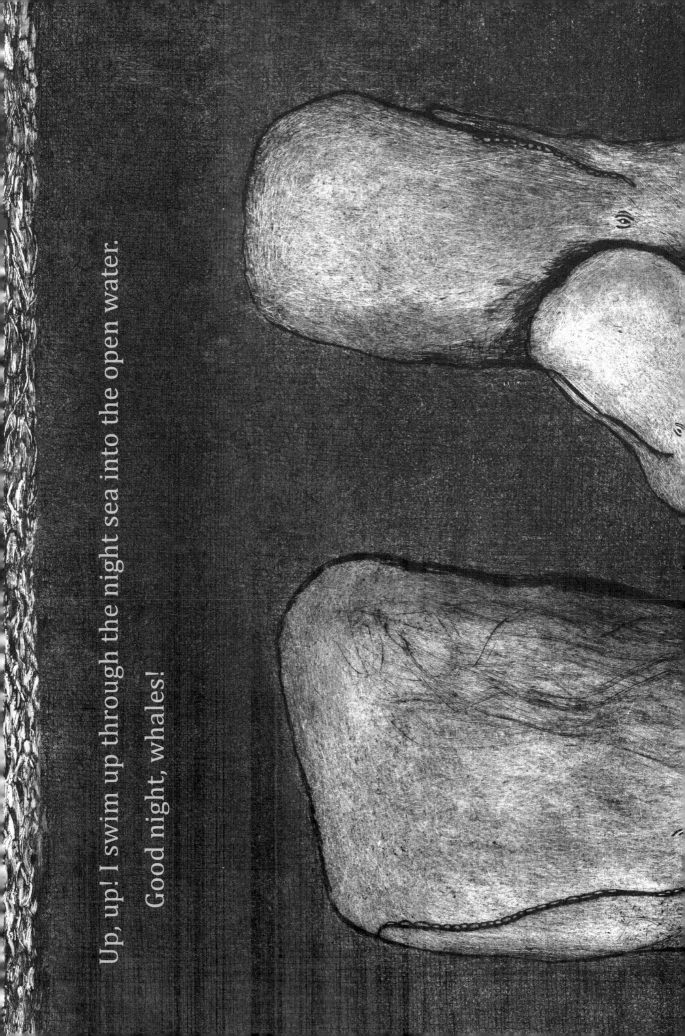

Up, up, up! I swim up through the night sea into the open water.

Good night, whales!

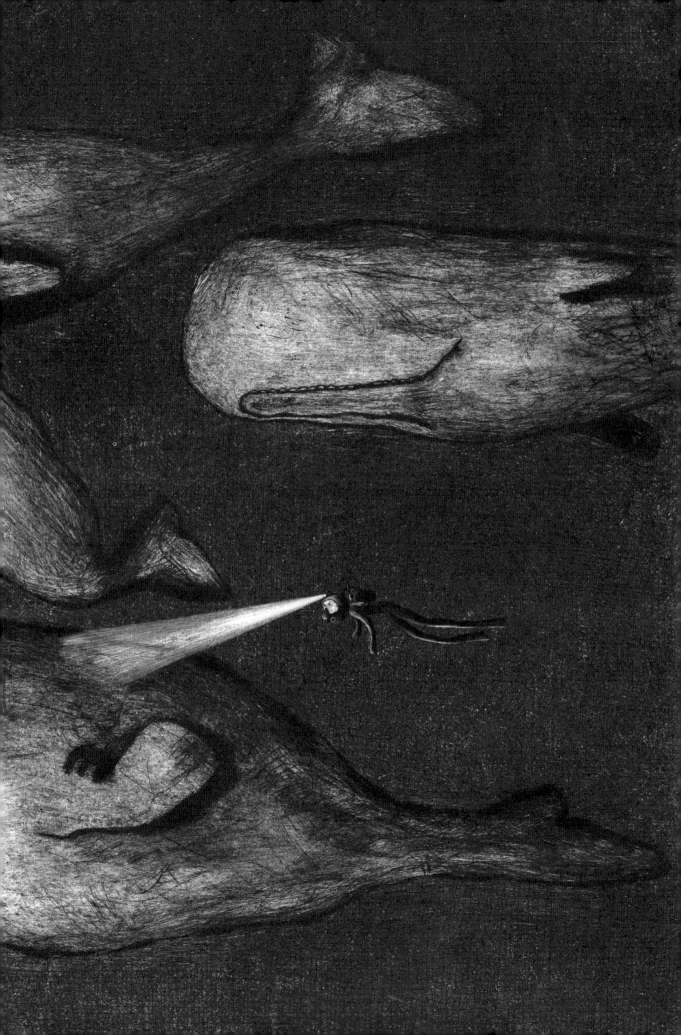

Back at the surface, I take a long deep breath.
The moon lights my way.

I whisper goodbye
and dream of the next time
I will dive, dive into the night sea.

For my best dive partner, Yan